Original title:
Chlorophyll Chronicles

Copyright © 2025 Creative Arts Management OÜ
All rights reserved.

Author: Eleanor Prescott
ISBN HARDBACK: 978-1-80581-825-0
ISBN PAPERBACK: 978-1-80581-352-1
ISBN EBOOK: 978-1-80581-825-0

Breathe Life into Green

In the garden, a leaf strikes a pose,
Whispering secrets to a curious rose.
"Hey there, buddy, I'm feeling so fine!"
"Got sunlight today? Let's sip some sunshine!"

The daisies giggle, they love the show,
While the grasshoppers jump, stealing the flow.
"Mind if we steal some of that breeze?"
"Only if you promise to dance with ease!"

The Language of Photosynthesis

Photosynthesis speaks in shades of green,
Sending out signals, crisp and serene.
The roots nod their heads, it's party time!
"Let's convert sunlight, it feels so sublime!"

Bubbles of oxygen rise with a cheer,
While beetles conclude they can't help but leer.
"Is that air fresh or just you?" they tease,
All while munching on some tasty leaves.

Ode to the Emerald Awakening

As dawn breaks gently, the greens arise,
Stretching their limbs toward clear blue skies.
Ferns whisper jokes that make ivy laugh,
"Why did the grass blade start a gaffe?"

"Because it wanted to be the life of the lawn,
But ended up tangled, all green and drawn!"
Laughter erupts from the bright marigolds,
"Join us, dear leaf, in our tales untold!"

Vignettes of Verdancy

A cucumber dreams of being a star,
While peas in pods plot adventures afar.
They giggle and squawk, sharing old pranks,
Trading tall tales of their earlier ranks.

The ivy lounges, a laid-back sage,
Telling young sprouts, "You'd better engage!"
"Sunshine's the ticket, so soak it all in,
And don't forget laughter; now that's how to win!"

The Archive of Botanical Wonders

In the garden of giggles, plants take a stand,
They dance with delight, swaying hand in hand.
Petunias prank daisies, what a sight to behold,
As ivy tells secrets that never get old.

With cacti as comedians, they poke and they jest,
While ferns hold their sides—this humor's the best.
Each leaf has a tale, a joke up its sleeve,
Beneath arching branches, they play and believe.

Green Legacy: A Nature's Diary

In the scribbles of sap, the trees laugh with glee,
Their rings tell a story, you won't want to flee.
The daisies are doodling, painting petals in pink,
As grass blades hum tunes, making creatures think.

The logs share their wisdom, but jesters they are,
With squirrels as scribes, racing fast and bizarre.
Each sprout holds a memory, a comic delight,
In nature's own journal, everything feels right.

Voice of the Leafy Spirits

In whispers of leaves, the spirits convene,
Spinning tales with the breeze, a playful machine.
The willows wiggle, like dancers you see,
While poplars gossip about you and me.

Their laughter erupts in the symphony bright,
With branches as microphones, they sing through the night.
A chorus of colors, what fun they can weave,
In the melody of nature, there's magic to believe.

Transmutations in the Forest Shade

In shadows where foliage makes pranks on the light,
Mushrooms pop up, giving fungi a fright.
A patchwork of humor paints roots underground,
Where laughter and fun in the soil can be found.

As pinecones fall gently, a tickle ensues,
The laughter of leaves, an echo of hues.
Beneath a sunbeam that twirls with delight,
The forest is chuckling, a jovial sight.

Woven Tales of Nature's Bounty

In a garden where veggies hold court,
The carrots in tights play a silly sport.
Radishes gossip with onions in rows,
While beans breakdance, in their flashy clothes.

The corn sings high and the peas hum low,
Potatoes do moonwalks, putting on a show.
Lettuce in sunglasses, chillin' in style,
While cucumbers giggle and wink with a smile.

Beneath the Whispering Leaves

Underneath branches where shadows flirt,
A chubby squirrel dons a tiny shirt.
He chats with the mushrooms, sharing old jokes,
While ferns giggle gently at pranking the folks.

The breeze carries whispers of secrets so grand,
Like flowers forming a rock band at hand.
With daisies on drums, and violets on bass,
This rural concert gives everyone space.

The Harmony of Sun and Shade

In the bright sun, the daisies dance,
But the shady ferns just dream and prance.
The sunflowers wave, as tall as can be,
While shadows play hide and seek with a bee.

With light-hearted giggles, the daisies shun,
The gloom of shade but join in the fun.
Every petal and leaf sings a silly refrain,
A merry melody, again and again.

Leafy Legends Unfolded

In the realm of trees, where stories grow,
A wise old oak just told a show.
With squirrels as actors and bugs as the crew,
Their comedy skits left everyone blue.

Beneath his branches, a tale spun bright,
Of raccoons at midnight, causing a fright.
As leaves crackle laughter in sways of delight,
Nature's fun secrets unfold in pure light.

Essence of the Evergreen

In the forest, trees wear pants,
Sprouting leaves with little prance.
The squirrels gossip, full of cheer,
While mossy banks hold tales to hear.

Pine cones tumble like old gents,
With funny hats and funny scents.
The ferns dance like they're in a show,
A leafy conga, all aglow.

Journeys Through the Glassy Green

In a garden where the weeds conspire,
A snail rides slowly, dreams of fire.
Each blade of grass a cushion soft,
As ladybugs take flight aloft.

They say the plants can tell a joke,
A pun or two, some leafy poke.
With every prick and every tick,
The green brigade grows bold and slick.

Whispers of the Wild Flora

The daisies chat beneath the sun,
Their little gossip's so much fun.
Each dandelion's a wish on spree,
Tickling bees and full of glee.

The orchids flaunt their colors bright,
In floral fashion, pure delight.
While vines entwine with gleeful shout,
In nature's world, there's no doubt.

The Palette of Nature's Brush

Nature's paintbrush splatters wide,
With every leaf, a brushy glide.
The colors dancing, vivid, bold,
In the green gallery, stories told.

From zany zinnias to chortling thyme,
Each flower winks, it's comedy time!
The shades of green are laughing too,
In the wild, the jokes are true.

Nature's Chromatic Whisper

In the garden where colors play,
Leaves giggle in the bright sun's ray.
A green leaf winks, oh what a tease,
While flowers shake like they're in a freeze.

Butterflies dance with such great flair,
Each one thinks they're a light-weight air.
A daisy boasts of its shiny head,
While roses pout, feeling underfed.

Squirrels chime in with their chitter chatter,
Claiming the nuts like they're the matter.
The sky joins in with a laughing hue,
As clouds drift by, all fuzzy and blue.

The Arbor's Tale

A mighty oak tells jokes from heights,
While crickets chime in with their insights.
"Why do leaves never get lost?" it grins,
"Because they always know where the fun begins!"

A pine tree snickers with a sticky smile,
"Ever seen a fern run a mile?"
And the birch joins in, it's such a hoot,
"They're rooted so deep, they'll never scoot!"

The trees have their roots in all the lore,
Of tales so tall, they could never bore.
Each twig has chimed in, with a pun or two,
In the shade, it's a comedy crew!

Lush Legacies

In the jungle, the vines compete,
For who can grow the fastest feet.
"Look at me swing, I'm like Tarzan!"
But branches just laugh, "You're a wannabe fan!"

The ferns whisper secrets of the past,
"Remember that time we grew so fast?
We won the race against the breeze,
While the flowers struggled, feeling the squeeze!"

Then a cactus chimed in, so bold and spry,
"Life's a prick, but I'm too cool to cry!"
While daisies and dandelions giggle bright,
Their laughter echoes through the starry night.

Under the Verdure Dome

Under the dome, where green dreams sway,
The plants play cards and dance all day.
"Who's the quickest to photosynthesize?"
They joke and tease, casting merry sighs.

A willow weeps but joins the fun,
She flips her branches, just trying to run.
Laughter spills from every leaf,
As roots exchange their playful mischief.

"Why did the petal refuse to bloom?
It found out flowers go 'ka-boom'!"
Amid chuckles and giggles, the day unwinds,
In this green castle, where fun always shines.

Secrets of the Sunlit Canopy

In the leafy heights above,
A squirrel dances, full of love.
He hides his nuts in plain sight,
Declaring it a gourmet fight.

The birds all chirp, they're such a mess,
Each thinks they're the star, I guess.
They argue how to swoop and dive,
Yet trip on branches, not so alive.

The sunbeams peek through the green,
While ants parade, they form a scene.
A marching band of tiny crew,
Their tiny hats, the perfect view.

With laughter ringing through the air,
The foliage sways without a care.
The secrets here in nature's chat,
Are best enjoyed with a friendly spat.

Tales from the Verdant Veil

In a forest thick, a tale unfolds,
Of a tree that dreams in greens and golds.
It whispers jokes to those who pass,
While casting shade with leafy sass.

The rabbits hop, they leap and bound,
In search of snacks they rarely found.
They nibble greens, then start to prance,
Inventing quite the bunny dance.

A snail's slow crawl, it takes all day,
While mockingbirds laugh, come what may.
They tease the slowpoke, 'You need a jet!'
But he just shrugs, 'I'm not done yet!'

The sun dips low, the night draws near,
With fireflies lighting up the cheer.
In this realm where stories blend,
Each leaf bears laughter, and joy won't end.

Lush Echoes of Summer

In summer's heat, the blossoms beam,
Each flower spills a silly dream.
Bees buzz around with endless glee,
As daisies declare, 'You can't catch me!'

A turtle slow, he hums a tune,
While frogs croak croon, beneath the moon.
They all compete for the best note,
As crickets laugh and start to gloat.

The sun shines bright on every face,
While shadows dance in a leafy race.
The blooms are grinning, stretching wide,
As beetles strut with leafy pride.

When raindrops fall, it's jump and splash,
With puddles forming, what a flash!
The laughter echoes, nature's play,
In this lush world, we laugh all day!

Symphony of the Swaying Leaves

In the canopy above, they sway,
Each leaf a dancer in the fray.
They whisper secrets, oh so bold,
While tangled vines play "Hide and Hold."

The woodpecker pecks with curious flair,
While chipmunks stockpile without a care.
They bicker over the last acorn,
While the wise old owl gives a yawn.

The shadows form a playful stage,
With fireflies glowing in a rage.
They challenge each other to a race,
As the garden smiles in pure embrace.

At sunset's call, the leaves applaud,
With rustling cheers, a welcome nod.
In this lush realm, the laughter weaves,
A symphony born from swaying leaves.

The Rhythm of Growth

In a garden where worms do cheer,
Bouncing plants that dance with glee.
Sunshine's tune draws them near,
While shadows hide the bumblebee.

Roots are tangled in a waltz,
Petals pirouette in style,
Nature's flair—no room for faults,
Each bloom shows off its greenish smile.

The gardener sings a silly song,
As daisies join the conga line.
Even weeds can't feel wrong,
Beneath the beams of sipping wine.

Laughter bubbles near the sprouts,
As critters join the funky beat.
In this world of colorful shouts,
Every leaf finds its tapping feet.

Legacy of the Leafy Tribe

In a forest of giggles and glee,
Where acorns boast of wisdom shared.
The leaves convene a jubilee,
As branches gossip without a care.

The elder oak tells tales so grand,
Of squirrels who conquer the skies.
With twinkling eyes, they all understand,
That roots hold the answers, oh my!

Frogs croak rhymes from the pond side,
While crickets chirp the leafy lore.
Their vibe is more than just pride,
It's laughter mixed with folklore.

As sunbeams tickle the youthful greens,
Every petal knows it's a blast.
The leafy tribe with its silly scenes,
Find joy in memories that last.

Leaves in the Wind

Swirling twirls, the leaves take flight,
Chasing breezes full of cheer.
Dancing haphazardly in delight,
While squirrels shout, "Look, we're here!"

A gust of laughter, a flip of green,
Leaves tumble, giggle, spin around.
With each pirouette, they're keen,
To share their jokes upon the ground.

Down they flutter, all askew,
Like jokers in a leafy play.
A conga line that never grew,
Just playful fun in a breezy ballet.

They'll chat about the windy days,
And how to ride that swirling tide.
In wind's embrace, they find their ways,
No need to hide, just glide, abide!

A Lexicon of Green Dreams

In a book where the cover's a leaf,
Words flutter like butterflies bright.
Chapters of sunshine and belief,
As plants dream under the moonlight.

Pages turn with a rustling sound,
Tales of veggies in splendid gowns.
Cucumbers dance on the ground,
While spinach tells jokes that astound.

With every word, there's a giggle,
In the stories that petals narrate.
From bushy shrubs to leafy wiggle,
Fables that celebrate fate.

So come take a peek in this tome,
Where greens have voices—loud and clear.
In the garden, all feel at home,
In this lexicon of joy and cheer.

Portraits of the Leafy Realm

In a kingdom of green, leaves wear crowns,
Dancing with laughter, they spin round and round.
Each leaf a comedian, tickling the breeze,
Joking with sunlight, sharing their tease.

The oak tells a tale, his bark all a-chuckle,
While the willow's long arms just wiggle and shuffle.
Pine cones play games, oh what a delight,
As squirrels chip in, making the scenes bright.

Dandelion dreams float up in a whirl,
Wishing they'd fly, those seeds all unfurl.
Grass blades giggle, brushing against toes,
While daisies and clovers throw fragrant rows.

And as night falls, with shadows that creep,
The leaves whisper secrets, but nowhere to sleep.
In this leafy realm, joy clips at the seams,
With humor and fun, they chase all their dreams.

The Pulse of the Green Heart

A rush of green beats in rhythm with glee,
Leaves shimmying softly, what a sight to see!
Vines twist and shout, chanting a tune,
While ferns wave their fronds, under the moon.

Ducks quack a duet, right by the pond,
While lily pads giggle, of lily they'll bond.
The thistle, so proud, preens in the sun,
Confidently claiming that they are the one.

A breeze kicks in, making leaves clap,
As ladybugs laugh with a tiny tap tap.
The garden's alive, with laughter to share,
Waving their greens, like they just don't care.

So join in the fun, take a leafy chance,
Nature's the stage for a vibrant dance.
Under this pulse, we all find delight,
With green hearts alive, oh what a night!

Beneath the Shade of Greatness

Beneath grand canopies, the shade is alive,
Where laughter and whispers make all creatures thrive.
A wise old oak chuckles, 'Do you see that squirrel?'
As he juggles his acorns, giving life a whirl.

The daisies gossip, sharing tales of bees,
While butterflies flutter, dancing with ease.
A picnic of shadows where friends gather 'round,
With leafy confetti falling all 'round the ground.

The breeze plays tag, tickling all it meets,
As trees spin tall stories, with whimsical beats.
The sun peeks through, like it's lost in the fun,
Casting giggles along till the day is done.

In this shade of greatness, the joy is immense,
With every branch swaying, it's nature's suspense.
So take off your shoes, let your laughter soar,
For under the leaves, there's always more!

Verses of the Vine

In a tangled garden, the vines weave their lore,
Spinning yarns of laughter, you'll beg for more.
They stretch and they twist, like dancers on stage,
Crafting funny stories, page after page.

A grape said to cherry, 'What's your secret?'
'Bouncing around, I'm always upbeat!'
The peas chuckle loudly, 'We're simply the best,
But let's not leaf out all the rest!

Pumpkins roll over, creating a scene,
With squash in the mix, they're all dressed in green.
Each vine has a story, a joke or two,
Growing their humor, like dew on the hue.

So join in the fun, beneath leafy vines,
Where laughter and joy mix in robust designs.
With nature's own pages, let the verses inspire,
For in this green world, we all laugh higher!

The Life of Lush

In the garden, plants do prance,
Wiggling leaves in a leafy dance.
Flowers gossip, colors bright,
Even weeds are feeling right!

Sunshine tickles every stem,
Dancing leaves, a photosynth gem.
Bees buzz in, taking their turn,
While ants march, with pride they churn.

Vegetables gossip in a row,
'Carrot, you're quite the show!'
Lettuce laughs, 'I'm not shy,'
As peas giggle, 'Watch us fly!'

In this patch of green delight,
Nature plots with sheer delight.
With worms as spies and beetles as jest,
Lush life blooms, a merry fest.

Chronicles of the Green Tapestry

Once upon a leafy spree,
Jungle vines played hide and seek.
Cacti bragged of sunny days,
While ferns rolled in the playful haze.

Roses winked, a flirty bunch,
Tattooed their petals in a crunch.
Thorns declared, 'We're tough as nails,'
While daisies shared their silly tales.

Oaks chuckled with mighty sway,
'We've been here, come what may.'
The clovers tossed a playful bet,
'Try to find us, we're not done yet!'

And so the plants in their green scheme,
Laughed and leaped, living the dream.
In every corner, joy did grow,
In this tapestry, life's vibrant show.

Roots and Resonance

In the soil, roots play charades,
Sharing secrets in leafy blades.
'Who pulled me down?' a carrot cried,
While potatoes sighed, 'It's quite a ride!'

Grab a drink! It's wormy wine,
A toast to the plants, so divine.
'We grow deep,' the sage does boast,
While radishes claim they host the most!

Bamboo stretches, grinning wide,
'Look at me, I'm full of pride!'
But mossy rocks just chuckle low,
'In this garden, you can't steal the show!'

From roots to crowns, in laughter we share,
Each plant a character, beyond compare.
Life's a giggle in green disguise,
Nature's jokes, a sweet surprise.

Swaying Sentinels

Tall trees stand like guards of glee,
Whispering tales to the honeybee.
With each breeze, a comic twist,
Branches dance, a wobbly list.

Swaying lilies take a bow,
While pansies ask, 'Who made you wow?'
Budget blooms laugh out loud,
'Not bad for a garden crowd!'

Saplings strut, feeling grown,
'Watch us, we've earned a throne!'
But daisies plead, 'We're not so small,'
'Together we're a floral ball!'

So here's to all in green attire,
Under the sun, we never tire.
With each chuckle, plants rejoice,
In their green kingdom, they have a voice.

Shadows and Sunbeams

In the garden, sunlight plays,
Dancing leaves in bright arrays.
They whisper jokes to bugs nearby,
While shadows giggle as they fly.

Sunbeams tease a dandelion,
"Bet you can't outshine a lion!"
The blossoms burst in laughter loud,
As bees form a buzzing crowd.

But when the evening starts to creep,
The leaves share secrets, soft and deep.
Oh, to be a leaf at night,
Cracking jokes under soft moonlight.

They stretch and yawn, they twist and bend,
Plotting mischief till day's end.
With every rustle, a punchline told,
Nature's humor, brave and bold.

Green Guardians

In the woods, the greens convene,
Guardians of glade, serene.
"Who's the funniest here of all?"
They argue by the towering wall.

A fern says, "I'm the whip-smart seed!"
The oak replies, "I'm here to lead!"
But whispers from the moss below,
"I'll win this contest, just watch me grow!"

They tell of roots that tickle toes,
And plants that wear outlandish clothes.
Amidst the giggles in their scheme,
They plot to prank the passing stream.

Through their laughter, joy does bloom,
Turning each glade into a room.
Where every leaf can find its worth,
These guardians laugh, reviving Earth.

The Language of Leaves

Leaves exchange whispers in the breeze,
"Did you hear that joke from the trees?"
One boasts of sunbathing all day,
While others laugh in a leafy ballet.

"I can rustle and make such sound!"
Said the maple, spinning round.
But the willow, with a swish and sway,
Retorts, "You can't dance like me, hooray!"

They play charades with shadows cast,
Entwined in laughter, ever vast.
From leaf to leaf, the humor spreads,
Even the squirrels warmly nod their heads.

In this green world, jesters thrive,
A giggling grove, so alive.
With every gust, their joys are weaved,
In the laughter of leaves, we all believed.

Fables of Photosynthesis

Once a ray of sunlight said,
"I'll tickle plants right on their head!"
The leaves giggled, soaking bright,
Drawing jokes from left and right.

They crafted tales of water's dance,
How roots would sway in a merry trance.
"With sugar and sunlight, we have our fun!"
Cried a sprout, basking in the sun.

Then came a cloud, all fluffy and wide,
Cracking jokes with no need to hide.
"Let's rain some puns to make you shine!"
And with each drop, the laughter aligned.

In this fable, the greens found glee,
Finding humor in their chemistry.
As the cycle spins with vibrant shine,
Every leaf knows how to intertwine.

Nature's Infinite Canvas

In the forest, colors collide,
Where squirrels in tutus try to hide.
Trees gossip in whispers so bold,
Of secrets and treasures, yet to unfold.

Dancing daisies wear crowns of dew,
A grasshopper donning a bright shade of blue.
Picnicking ants, a feast for the ants,
While a mischievous raccoon steals the chance!

Lemonade clouds float by, oh so sweet,
While tulips break into a funny beat.
Nature's painting is never quite still,
A canvas alive, bursting with thrill.

Verdant Meditations

Frogs with hats sit, talking philosophy,
Where every leaf is a new epiphany.
Moss holds court on a rock so spry,
While clouds laugh above in the big, blue sky.

Daisies debate what's in style this year,
While worms in shades cheer and persevere.
The sun smiles wide at their curious spree,
As laughter of nature rings wild and free.

A butterfly twirls like a prima ballerina,
With flowers that sway, offering a subpoena.
In every corner, a giggle or shout,
In this garden of glee, there is no doubt!

The Chronicles of Leaf Shadows

Under the trees, shadows dance and sway,
As beetles play games in their own funny way.
With each step, the floor crunches with glee,
Nature's own carpet, made just for me.

Vines twist and tangle, a circus delight,
While owls snicker softly, planning their flight.
The breeze tells tales of the mischief unspoken,
Of flowers that giggle, their patience is broken.

A woodpecker's drumming joins in the fun,
While butterflies race, each a colorful run.
In the leafy shadows, joy's always near,
A captivating world where whimsy appears.

Gifts of the Green World

From acorns to apples, a banquet unfolds,
With snakes in bow ties, oh how they uphold!
Berries wear hats of bright, merry hues,
While daisies gossip in their dainty shoes.

The caterpillar's fashion show goes afoot,
While beetles march proudly in their slick suit.
Laughter rises like steam from a pot,
In the garden of giggles, it's a jubilant lot!

With every raindrop, a tickle or tease,
Nature's been busy crafting joy with ease.
In this green world, there's no time to stall,
Just smiles and laughter, gifts shared by all.

Echoes of Evergreen

In a forest full of sass,
The trees wear glasses, looking brash.
They gossip with the morning dew,
And dance with squirrels who paint their view.

The pines hold rhythm with a sway,
While moss joins in their leafy play.
A bumblebee serves as their DJ,
Turning every dull day into a cabaret.

The laughter rises, oh so bright,
As acorns drop, it's quite a sight.
A rabbit slips, then takes a bow,
Declaring, 'I'm the star of now!'

So join the fun, come take a seat,
In this green kingdom, life's a treat.
The trees will sing, the flowers cheer,
Join in the antics, bring your beer!

Ties that Bind the Soil

Worms in tuxedos underground,
Movin' in class, with style profound.
They twist and twirl, a wiggly show,
Rooting for greens, they steal the show.

Roses roll their eyes, so prim,
Stiff competition? They can't be grim.
"I'm the beauty," they claim with pride,
While daisies giggle, "We're on this ride!"

Underneath the party, roots entwine,
Sharing secrets, 'It's your turn to shine!'
Fungi whisper, 'Let the fun begin,'
With a hearty laugh, they throw it in.

In this soil, life's also a jest,
Each plant and creature, feeling blessed.
So raise a leaf to this goofy crew,
They'll keep the stories fresh and new!

The Palette of the Forest

In a forest where colors collide,
Crayons of nature take joy in their ride.
A bluebird squeaks, 'I'm the true blue!'
While daisies pout, 'Look at us too!'

The sunflowers sway, all bright and bold,
Telling stories of petals they hold.
A splash of red, a wink of green,
Every shade has a joke, if seen!

Fluffy clouds hang out, playing tag,
Stealing hues from a ladybug's rag.
Together they paint, skies wide and clear,
Who knew colors had so much cheer?

Join the brush in this vibrant spree,
Where laughter blooms on every tree.
Nature's canvas is a feast of delight,
In this quirky world, everything feels right!

Harmonies of Herbaceous Dreams

In garden beds, where whispers hum,
Herbs throw parties, oh what fun!
Basil brings guacamole to the show,
While cilantro salsa starts to flow.

Rosemary strums on a twiggy lute,
Thyme joins along, a seasoned hoot.
They sway and spin, a leafy band,
Gathered around, we take a stand.

Minty fresh, with a twist of lime,
A cocktail of giggles, perfectly rhyme.
Oregano casts a spicy spell,
While chives giggle at the stories they tell.

So come and join this herbal dream,
Where laughter flows like a bubbling stream.
In every leaf, a chuckle is grown,
In this jolly garden, you'll never be alone!

The Green Saga Unfolds

In a garden so lush, where the weeds play tricks,
The plants throw a party, with wild rubber picks.
A cucumber in shades, trying hard to impress,
Declared, "I'm the coolest!" in his leafy dress.

The daisies giggle, with petals so wide,
As the carrots conspire, in their underground pride.
A tomato rolls over, a sight oh so bold,
"I'm juicy and ripe, but still green, behold!"

The bees start to buzz, with a drink in their cup,
While the broccoli joins in, forcing others to sup.
In this veggie ballet, they twist and sway,
Who knew plants could party in such a fun way?

As twilight approaches, the showmed surely,
With fireflies dancing, their glow kinda swirly.
"Let's dance till the dawn!" all the herbs chant loud,
In this green saga, they've made quite a crowd.

Sustain the Green

The lettuce squeaks softly, a crisp little sound,
As the spinach plays tunes, with rhythm profound.
The peas pop with laughter, as they trip on their dew,
"Let's keep it all green!" they squeal and pursue.

A fern tells the tale of a plot twist most strange,
Where two cactus fell in love, oh what a change!
A sunflower spins, with a dance quite absurd,
While the pine trees just giggle at every lost word.

The carrots conduct, with nods of their green heads,
While the radishes shout, "No more turning red!"
In a world full of color, they all found a scene,
Where being a bit silly is the best way to beam.

And so they all cheer, with voices like sprout,
"Let's flaunt every green, and skip every doubt!"
For in the embrace of this playful brigade,
They know with a grin, the green has it made.

Green Whispers of the Forest

In the whispering woods, leaves gossip away,
A squirrel with style, in dramatic display.
"Are those acorns new?" coos a chipmunk nearby,
As the trees roll their eyes, with a rustling sigh.

The mushrooms are chatting, their caps all aglow,
With promises of rain in a dance for the show.
Fungi declare, with a wink and a glee,
"Hey, let's get this mixed-up party with tea!"

The foxes prance 'round, in their bright orange coats,
While the owls hoot jokes, with wise, funny notes.
"Why did the leaf fall?" a young bird sings sweet,
"To join in the fun, oh! It just had to greet!"

In a whirl of the green, they all find their groove,
With laughter and chatter that makes the trees move.
So dance through the forest, where fun seekers play,
In whispers of green, we'll brighten your day!

The Dance of Leaf and Light

The leaves start to sway, in a sunlight jig,
As shadows play tag, in a bright leafy gig.
The sunbeams are tickled, in a shimmering race,
While the branches join in, with a rustling grace.

A flower declares, with a twirl and a spin,
"I'm the belle of the ball; let the light in!"
With each burst of color, a giggle, a gleam,
As the petals all bloom in a sunny daydream.

The wind plays the music, as small critters cheer,
While the daisies nudge in, with a light, happy beer.
"Come dance with us, friends! Let's jive with delight,
In this marvelous show of leaf and light!"

So gather the green, and embrace all your sight,
With the joy of the day making everything bright.
For in this wild dance, oh how spirits delight,
Each leaf, each petal, in a silly spotlight.

Vibrations Under the Canopy

In a forest full of giggles, leaves sway,
The trees gossip secrets in a merry play.
Squirrels wear sunglasses, so cool and bright,
While birds chirp jokes, from morning till night.

Frogs in bowties leap with flair,
Dancing roots, they bounce through the air.
A breeze tickles ferns, they start to shake,
Even the mushrooms know how to break.

A worm in a top hat, round and spry,
Winks at a snail zooming right by.
Nature's comedy, oh what a sight,
Greenery laughing under golden light.

Through twinkling leaves, the humor swirls,
In the wild theater, it joyfully twirls.
All around, the laughter flows like streams,
In this vibrant world, we dance in dreams.

Dance of the Verdant Spirits

The grasses hold hands in a spirited cheer,
While blossoms spin tales that all can hear.
A beetle in tap shoes takes to the stage,
With a ladybug clapping, they're quite the rage.

In the shade of a tree, a party ignites,
Where ants take the floor, showing their might.
Jumping for joy, they twirl and they leap,
Weaving through roots, in a rhythm so deep.

Oh, the daisies giggle, what a wild scene,
As mischievous vines stretch at the green screen.
A sunbeam peeks in, with a wink and a grin,
Inviting the night, let the fun times begin.

So join in the dance, shed your worries tight,
With every leaf rustle, it feels just right.
Nature's joyful party is never a bore,
Under the wide sky, who could ask for more?

Timeless Green Embrace

Amidst the greens, a raccoon plays tricks,
While coyotes howl with their clever licks.
Moss blankets laughter, spread far and wide,
As shadows stretch out to the bright sunlight.

With vines like ropes, they pull you in,
To a world of whimsy and cheeky sin.
The apples giggle, so plump and round,
While cherries trade stories without a sound.

At each turn in this emerald maze,
Every shrub or flower comes with a craze.
A breeze tells a joke as it dances by,
With leaves nodding 'yes' to the humor nearby.

In this timeless nook, the joy does abide,
Welcoming all with arms open wide.
So come join the fun, leave worries behind,
In the heart of the green, true bliss you will find.

Echoes of Growth and Change

The whispers of leaves sing songs of delight,
As the sun dips low, embracing the night.
In a puddle nearby, frogs practice their lines,
While crickets compose their sweet serenades and signs.

A caterpillar dons a wig made of fluff,
Saying, "Just wait, this transformation's tough!"
While daisies wear crowns, strutting their stuff,
Life in the green is playfully rough.

The wise old oak chuckles deep from his core,
Sharing with saplings, tales of yore.
Every breeze carries laughter through dense lace,
A tapestry woven in nature's embrace.

From the tiniest sprout to the broadest tree,
Each creature within feels the wild jubilee.
So join in the echoes of change and of cheer,
In the ever-growing joy, you'll find us all here.

Shadows Beneath the Foliage

In the shade where critters dwell,
A squirrel tells a nutty tale.
Leaves giggle as the breeze does sway,
Be careful not to trip, I say!

A bug on a leaf holds a dance,
But poof! There goes his chance!
He slips and lands in a puddle,
Now he's in a leafy muddle!

The shadows whisper silly pranks,
A toad jumps in with flips and flanks.
All the plants laugh, what a scene!
Who knew shade could be so keen?

From ferns to flowers, laughter flows,
Each leaf has secrets, who really knows?
In this hood of green, we play around,
With giggles hidden in the ground!

The Heartbeat of the Grove

The trees sway and play the tune,
Beneath the light of the big round moon.
A dance-off starts, who will win?
A twiggy hip-hop with lots of spin!

In the grove, where laughter thrives,
A fox in sunglasses high-fives.
A punchline heard from roots so deep,
Even the owls try not to peep!

Rabbits judge the leafy show,
While fireflies put on a glow.
Nature's jesters in every shade,
With jokes as sharp as autumn blades.

An acorn roars, "I'm not afraid!"
The oak replies, "Well, that's well-played."
Each heartbeat in this green abode,
Is laughter shared along the road!

Radiance in Every Blade

In every leaf, laughter glows,
As sunlight tickles the undergrowth.
A dance party starts on the lawn,
Where blades of grass greet the dawn!

A dandelion puffs a joke,
About a bug that tried to poke.
"Sir, you're dressed like a tiny clown!"
And everyone laughs as he falls down!

Bamboo sways, it's got quick moves,
While daisies play with their grooves.
Pollen's a sprinkle of fun, it seems,
Bringing joy in yellow streams.

Together they laugh, basking in light,
Nature's party feels just right.
In this patch of green and gold,
Every blade shares stories bold!

Chronicles of the Leafy Realm

In a realm where green tales are spun,
A caterpillar rolls for fun.
"Hey, leaf! I'm the king, can't you see?"
The leaf just shakes, "That's not quite me!"

Beneath the branches, gossip swirls,
"Did you hear about the acorn pearls?"
The tree trunk scoffs, "That can't be true!"
While mushrooms giggle, "We'll take two!"

Even snails have tales to share,
Gliding slowly with style and flair.
"Watch me slide with a glitter trail!"
Leaves chuckle, "Your speed's a fail!"

The chorus of green sings jokes and glee,
In this leafy realm, wild and free.
So come and join the fun today,
In every leaf, laughter leads the way!

When the Forest Speaks

When the trees start to chatter,
You'd think they've just won the splatter.
Branches waving, leaves take flight,
Hoping to win the title of 'Most Bright'.

Frogs croak in a plumbing debate,
While squirrels claim the forest's fate.
Mushrooms gossip with a sly grin,
"Did you see who tripped on that bin?"

Barkly trees in a fashion show,
Wearing moss like a funky throw.
A breeze blowing laughter so free,
As nature giggles in jubilee.

Even the soil has jokes to share,
Wink at the flowers, who throw high air.
Dancing with vines, a wild charade,
In this forest of fun, none can invade.

The Embrace of Green Light

Sunshine throws its green confetti,
Frogs in tuxedos, feeling quite petty.
Bouncing off leaves in a playful show,
Nature's own disco, stealing the flow.

Dandelions burst with sheer delight,
Whispering secrets up into the night.
The daisies giggle, oh, what a tease,
As bumblebees hum their sweet little sneeze.

The sunlight flirts with a mossy patch,
While crickets play tunes, a perfect match.
Fireflies dance in their glow-worm suits,
Reveling in this floral hoot.

Even the ferns are feeling so bold,
Telling the stories that never get old.
In this wacky world of greenery trim,
We laugh at nature, and she laughs with whim.

Murmurs of the Ancient Trees

Old oaks whisper, 'What's the scoop?'
While pine needles join in the loop.
With each rustle and creak they make,
The squirrels snicker and start to shake.

"Did you hear about the bush that cried?"
"Yeah, it's got feelings, can't be denied!"
Leaves stealing glances, oh what a thrill,
While roots wiggle in time with the hill.

A beetle tells jokes about life on a log,
And mushrooms laugh, "Stop being a frog!"
The canopy giggles, filtering light,
As shadows sway, causing a fright.

But beneath all the chuckles, calmness reigns,
In nature's laughter, joy still remains.
With trees giving lessons on how to live free,
The murmurs grow louder, come sit by me.

Enchanted by Green Hues

In a world painted with vibrant green,
Every leaf is a dazzling queen.
They sway and twirl, flaunting their charms,
While bees buzz around, spreading good farms.

Grass tickles toes in playful tease,
As sunlight dances through the leaves with ease.
A rabbit grins, sporting a hat,
"This isn't just grass, it's a luxury mat!"

The flower beds hold a fashion spree,
Roses and lilies sipping herbal tea.
A moth in a tux, flutters and bows,
"Nature is wild, and here's my vows!"

With the breeze whispering not to fret,
Embrace every hue, let's not forget.
In this enchanted green, life's full of cheer,
Come join the fun, let's all gather near.

Emerald Veins of the Earth

In the garden, plants do sway,
With a little dance, they greet the day.
Worms hold parties underground,
Groovin' to the earth's soft sound.

Frogs in hats, beetles with flair,
Host a concert, everyone's there!
Grass blades giggle in the breeze,
Tickled by a fluttering sneeze.

Moss wears slippers, all so snug,
While roots embrace, sharing a hug.
Sunshine drips from every leaf,
Their humorous tales bring pure relief.

Roots gossip about the rain,
"Did you hear? It's coming again!"
A leaf threw shade, and oh what fun,
Nature's laughter — we all run!

The Tapestry of Living Green

A patchwork quilt of green delight,
Where plants prance in pure sunlight.
Vines like serpents, all entwined,
Whisper secrets, so maligned.

Daisy chains dispute their fame,
"I'm prettier!" they all exclaim.
Toadstools chuckle, stacked so high,
With mushrooms wearing wigs that fly.

Caterpillars with dreams to fly,
Worry 'bout their lunch — oh my!
Butterflies tease them, flitting about,
"Complain less, just change your route!"

A squirrel wrote a novel, bold,
Of acorn heists and tales retold.
Leaves blush in various hues,
Giggling at nature's funny views.

Hidden Stories of the Underbrush

Tiny critters roam around,
In the underbrush, where fun is found.
Ants in suits hold a meeting grand,
Debating crumbs from the promised land.

Mice in shorts race past the stones,
While snails take bets with squeaky tones.
Chipmunks jest over a nutty prize,
With a wink and grin, oh how time flies!

Fungi wear cloaks, a fancy show,
Hosting meetings with roots below.
Bushes gossip, leaves listen tight,
Nature's theatrics, such a sight!

A spider spins tales oh so vast,
Of adventures that happen so fast.
In the underbrush, laughter reigns,
Where fun grows wild, forget the pains!

Serenity in Green Reflections

Rippling waters mirror the skies,
Where lily pads play, and dance, and rise.
Fishes flip in a comedic show,
While frogs croak lines that steal the glow.

Willow trees sway and nod their heads,
Keeping secrets that nature spreads.
A dragonfly zips with stylish spin,
While a turtle grins, slow and thin.

Pond lilies yawn in morning light,
Sharing dreams of a sweet flight.
Beetles race on a watery stage,
Chasing reeds — an endless page!

Sunbeams laugh at shadows' plight,
In the garden, all feels right.
Nature's mirth, a joyful stream,
Where every leaf fulfills a dream!

Songs of the Brooding Forest

In deep woods where shadows loom,
The squirrels dance like they're in bloom.
The trees gossip with rustling leaves,
While mushrooms plot mischief, oh how they tease!

A raccoon wears a crown of twigs,
Declaring dinner with clever jigs.
The forest floor, a stage so grand,
With critters performing on leafy land.

A wise owl chuckles, head held high,
Saying, "Life's a show, just give it a try!"
With frogs in tuxedos, they croak a tune,
Under a chandelier made of the moon.

So if you tread where the wild things play,
Join in the fun, don't just pass by today!
The brooding forest with laughter loud,
Is where even the shy can stand proud.

The Mystique of Growing Things

In a garden where veggies put on a show,
A carrot whispers to a shy tomato,
"I'm long and orange, a crunchy delight,"
While onions disguise in their layers tight.

The peas crack jokes, their pods all a-glow,
"We're the greenest snacks, don't you know?"
With beans climbing high, reaching for sun,
It's a botanical circus, oh what fun!

Herbs join the party with scents so divine,
Basil's a bard, and mint's quite the whine.
They flirt with the bees, buzzing in mirth,
In this verdant realm, life's bursting with worth.

So tiptoe through blossoms, join in the cheer,
For every growing thing holds laughter near.
With sprouting smiles and roots that sing,
Isn't it lovely, the joy plants bring?

Reveries Among the Green

In fields of grass, where nimble sprites play,
Sunbeams tickle, driving gloom away.
Blades of green begin to sway,
As butterflies dance, brightening the day.

A dandelion dreams of becoming a star,
While daisies gossip, giggling from afar.
The breeze carries secrets, whispers on high,
As clovers make wishes, catching the sky.

In this lush realm, with crunch and cheer,
Funny faces grow throughout the year.
With every giggle, the petals unfold,
Tales of the green become laughter retold.

So join the revelry, all joy in the scene,
Where nature plays tricks that are silly and keen.
Among the green, let your spirit take flight,
For every laugh is a joy in the light.

Echoing the Earth's Lullaby

The soil hums softly, a rhythm so sweet,
Where worms hold concerts beneath our feet.
They wiggle and jiggle, in dirt they convene,
The underground band that you've rarely seen.

Trees sway gently, their branches will sway,
With leaves that clap hands, in a leafy ballet.
The wind joins in, whistling a tune,
As critters dance 'neath the silvered moon.

In the meadows, the grasshoppers sing,
With crickets chirping, a jovial string.
A symphony of life, we hear it so clear,
This merry orchestra brings us all cheer.

So let's sway together to Earth's gentle voice,
In every rustle, let's make some noise!
For in nature's laughter, we find our bliss,
In the echoing lullaby, we can't help but kiss.

Sagas of the Silent Grove

In the grove where whispers cheer,
Trees gossip about the deer.
Moss tickles squirrels in a race,
While crickets hold a singing space.

Dancing shadows, leaves all shuffle,
Bugs in bow ties start to shuffle.
A snail spins tales with such delight,
Of midnight snacks and starry night.

Ferns wear hats, so dapper and bright,
Rabbits giggle at the sight.
Frogs give speeches, bold and grand,
While fireflies don their lighting band.

At dusk, the moon takes off its hat,
And sings a lullaby to the cat.
With laughter echoing 'round the trees,
Nature's jokes, carried by the breeze.

Nature's Chromatic Legacy

In a patch of plaid where daisies bloom,
Bees debate who gets the room.
A rainbow twists on a breeze,
As petals dance with utmost ease.

The sun throws paints across the sky,
While butterflies boldly fly.
Mushrooms giggle in tall grass,
Telling secrets no one can pass.

Caterpillars plotting their flight,
Dreaming of wings with all their might.
A ladybug takes up the cause,
Whispering funny, tiny jaws.

As twilight falls, colors unite,
With crickets chirping through the night.
Nature smiles with joy and flair,
In a world that's vibrant and rare.

The Enchantment of Dappled Light

In sunbeams where the shadows sway,
A chipmunk cracks a nut ballet.
Light and dark play peek-a-boo,
While the brook hums a silly tune.

Dancing dust in golden rays,
Makes the ants go wild for days.
A spider spins a web of glee,
Holding parties under a tree.

Squirrels wear their acorn hats,
Chasing shadows and teasing cats.
Glimmers flicker, laughter sings,
In a realm of fantastic things.

As dusk arrives, the colors blend,
With giggles low on every bend.
Nature whispers, "Join the fun!"
As day and night become as one.

Melodies of the Mossy Path

Along the path where mushrooms play,
A gnome hums his merry way.
Fungi tap dance on the floor,
While elves sneak snacks from nature's store.

The moss provides a comfy seat,
For rabbits sharing tales so sweet.
Worms recite their poetry,
As nature's chorus sings with glee.

A hedgehog strums a tiny lute,
While daisies shake their neighbor's root.
In the background, trees applaud,
For every joke and blessing bestowed.

As starlight twinkles in the deep,
Nature nods; its secrets keep.
With every note and soft refrain,
The forest laughs, without a strain.

Emerald Echoes

In the garden, plants are gabbing,
Spouting tales, it's quite a blabbing.
A leaf sneezed, the others cheered,
"Watch out for bugs! They've all appeared!"

A sunflower jokes, with head held high,
"I'm not just pretty, I can fly!"
Dandelions giggle, seeds in tow,
"We're the fluffiest, just so you know!"

The ferns shake hands, in nature's hall,
With roots like gossip, they grow tall.
"Did you hear about the tree's great fall?
It landed softly – a real leaf brawl!"

So stroll along this leafy scene,
Where nature's laughter is evergreen!
With every breeze, there's chatter, too,
In this green world, where jokes ensue!

The Green Veins of Life

In a forest full of silly trees,
They gossip 'bout the latest breeze.
A squirrel whispers, tail so spry,
"Last night I saw a bird that tried to fly!"

Grass blades gossip, low and sneaky,
"Why do we tickle toes? It's cheeky!"
While vines entwine, they share the news,
"Did you see that frog with polka dot shoes?"

Leaves on branches start a choir,
"Sing with me, let's start a fire!"
But not real fire, just the fun,
Of nature's dusk, when day is done!

So listen close, that giggling sound,
In this green world where joy is found.
Through every root, and bud so spry,
Nature's humor will never die!

Whispers of the Canopy

High above in the leafy splendor,
The branches chat 'bout the latest sender.
A breeze slips in, they start a dance,
"Hey, did you catch that last glance?"

A wise old oak grins, wide and grand,
"Told a twig to lend a hand.
But it just stood there, stiff and tall,
I guess not all can join the ball!"

Down below, the bushes band,
Telling stories of the mischievous sand.
"Last week, it tickled my roots so sweet,
I thought I'd burst – what a silly feat!"

So sway and spin in this leafy hush,
Where laughter blooms in every brush.
In the canopy, where whispers blend,
Nature's chuckles never end!

Leafy Legends

Once a leaf claimed, with quite a stir,
"I've got the secret, I'm quite a blur!"
But when the wind began to blow,
It twirled around, and to the ground did go!

A fern, so proud, stood tall and lush,
"I dance with grace, I never rush!"
Yet tripped on dew, it flopped about,
"Oi, I swear I'll never pout!"

The flowers gather for a tale,
Of bees that come when their scents prevail.
"Did you see that clumsy bee?"
"It bumped the rose, just to be free!"

So in this garden, full of glee,
Nature spins tales, with giddy spree.
Each leaf a legend in the sun,
Funny stories have just begun!

The Dance of Leaf and Light

In the sun's warm embrace, they twist and sway,
Leaves giggle softly, a bright ballet.
Twirling and shaking, they catch their fun,
Each leaf a dancer, under the sun.

With a whispering breeze, their laughter flies,
Chasing their shadows, no need for disguise.
Ambassadors of green, they tease and play,
In a world of humor, they brighten the day.

Verdant Visions

The garden's a stage, where green dreams prance,
Each stem has a story, each leaf does a dance.
Bursts of bright laughter, as petals all cheer,
Nature's own comedy, let's give a cheer!

Riddles of roots and their shenanigans, too,
Plotting their mischief under skies so blue.
A party of ferns in a leafy charade,
Dancing on earth, their mischief displayed.

From Sap to Sky

Sapsuckers giggle in tree tops so high,
Chasing the sunlight, their spirits don't die.
With every drip drop, they start to conspire,
Planting their jokes, sending skies into fire.

From roots to the crown, they share their delight,
Making the clouds giggle, painting them bright.
Nature's own jesters, beneath every dome,
They bring a lush laughter that feels like home.

The Symphony of Sunlit Leaves

Leaves rustle a tune, a hilarious sound,
Bouncing in rhythm, they dance all around.
With every wind gust, they chuckle and jest,
Nature's own band, bringing joy to the rest.

The sun plays piano, the shadows attend,
A whimsical concert that never will end.
Roots stomp in unison, branches align,
Creating a masterpiece, weaves humor divine.

The Alchemy of Green

A leaf sat upon a park bench,
With dreams of becoming a rich, fine wrench.
It whispered with envy to the sun,
"I'd shine like gold if I just had fun!"

The trees rolled their eyes, oh what a fuss,
They chuckled and said, "Join the bus!"
"Let's mix some laughter with a breeze,
And turn your stardom into cheese!"

One day it sprouted a grin so wide,
With hopes that the breeze would take it for a ride.
But the wind just giggled, 'You silly green chap,
You're destined for shadows, now take a nap!"

Yet still it shimmered, bright and spry,
Chasing butterflies fluttering by.
So here's to the leaf who dared to dream,
And found his fortune in a whimsical scheme!

Sun-Kissed Tales from the Woods

In the woods where sunlight spills,
Lived a squirrel with a suitcase of thrills.
He packed up jokes and a nut or two,
Declaring, "I'm off to join the crew!"

He pranced past mushrooms in silly shoes,
Singing songs about the fog and the dew.
The owls hooted, 'What's this ruckus about?'
'Just a squirrel who's dreaming! No need to pout!"

With every step, he'd tell a tale,
Of dancing flowers and a buddy snail.
They'd have a ball beneath the moon,
While stars chimed in, playing a tune!

So if you wander where shadows gleam,
Remember the squirrel and his glorious dream.
Laugh with the leaves and join in the jest,
In the sun-kissed woods, it's always a fest!

Roots of the Earth's Memory

Deep in the earth, the roots had a chat,
Discussing the weather and a curious cat.
'Did you see the owl wearing a hat?'
'Oh yes, and it looked as posh as a brat!'

They chuckled at flowers, such showy displays,
While wiggles of worms crept in silly ways.
'Let's start a band, we'll call it The Soil,'
'And serenade beings who dig, plant, or toil!'

With each little giggle, they wriggled with glee,
While dreaming of concerts beneath the old tree.
The daisies agreed to join in on the beat,
As beetles volunteered to dance on their feet.

So roots of the earth found they could have fun,
In a world where the sun sparked a wild run.
Life's a festival, with no cause to frown,
Just ask the old roots, they'll never back down!

Dreaming in Shades of Green

In a forest of dreams, shades of green play,
A chameleon chuckled, 'It's my fashion today!'
He flipped through colors as quick as a flash,
Till he landed in turquoise, oh what a splash!

Nearby, the ferns rolled in playful delight,
Telling tales of the grasshopper's hilarious flight,
They giggled about squirrels who danced on a whim,
And the mushroom that tried to sing like a hymn!

As the sunlight splattered across leafy ground,
Everyone joined in, the laughter profound.
From tall trees to tiny, each big belly shook,
In a festival of green, no one was forsook!

So if you wander 'neath the emerald glow,
Join the party where the laughter flows.
Dream in hues that are bold and bright,
And dance, dear friend, in the soft moonlight!

Secrets in the Shade

In the forest where shadows dance,
Leaves whisper secrets with a chance.
A squirrel in a tux, looking quite dapper,
Jokes about acorns, it's quite the caper.

Mushrooms giggle, wearing their hats,
While crickets play tunes with their tiny bats.
A toad croaks puns, ribbits in glee,
The shade tells tales, come sit with me!

Bees with sunglasses, buzzing around,
Pollinating humor, spreading it sound.
Beneath the old oak, life's a great jest,
In the green solitude, we laugh with the best.

So if you wander, take this in stride,
In the shade's embrace, let laughter reside.
For nature's a jester, full of surprise,
With smiles in the leaves, and laughter that flies.

Tales of the Verdant Heart

In the depths of the woods, where the wild things are,
A frog sings opera, it's the weirdest star.
With twigs for a baton, he leads the show,
In tales of the green, hilarity flows.

The trees share gossip with creaky old stumps,
About a raccoon who stole the last chumps.
He dances and prances, a thief on the run,
All while the owls hoot, 'This is such fun!'

A flower sneezes, petals in the wind,
While worms tell stories, their humor unpinned.
With laughter as currency, the forest will thrive,
In the heart of the green, everyone's alive!

So let's raise our glasses to vines that entwine,
To the chuckles and giggles, oh how they shine!
Each leaf has a tale, each root has a part,
In this funny saga of the verdant heart.

Nature's Green Story

In a meadow of mischief, where daisies splay,
A butterfly bobbles, hip-hop all day.
With colors so bright, it's hard not to smile,
Nature's own jester, spreading joy mile by mile.

A rabbit in shades, with a carrot in hand,
Claims to be the best DJ in the land.
The thumping of bunnies, grooving till night,
In this green story, everything's light!

Wildflowers frolic, their petals in bloom,
While the grasshoppers gather, rehearsing their tune.
A parrot nearby, with an amusing flair,
Cracks jokes with a grin, spreading joy in the air.

So skip through the fields, embrace the delight,
For nature's green story is a comical sight.
With laughter as seeds, in this vibrant retreat,
Every chuckle and grin turns the world sweet.

Hues of Harmony

In a garden of giggles, where colors collide,
The sunflowers chatter with nothing to hide.
There's a rumor of rainbows, painting the sky,
With pastel punsters who flutter on by.

A hedgehog in sneakers, racing a snail,
Both argue who's fastest, it's an epic tale.
The petals are clapping in harmony bright,
As laughter blossoms, taking joyous flight.

Bumblebees buzzing with choreographed moves,
Try to impress with their fancy grooves.
With nectar as rhythm, they circle and twirl,
In this vibrant dance of the natural world.

So gather round friends, let's share in the cheers,
For in hues of harmony, joy conquers fears.
Each stitch of color, a giggle or two,
In the garden's embrace, we'll laugh, me and you!

The Spirit of the Green Path

In the garden where the weeds play,
A carrot pretends it's a gourmet buffet.
With lettuce laughs and tomato cheer,
They throw a party that smells quite dear.

The radishes dance with pickles in tow,
They groove in the dirt, all set to show.
While peas pod-roll like they own the scene,
Proud of their green, oh so evergreen!

But then comes the rabbit, all sly and sweet,
He hops into chaos, ready to eat.
The veggies scatter, giggles ensue,
A funny fiasco in morning dew!

So carry on, little veggies so spry,
In your leafy world, just aim for the sky.
With roots in the soil and giggles in bloom,
You're the spirit of fun in your lovely green room!

Reflections Through the Canopy

Under leaves where the sunlight gleams,
A squirrel plots with nutty schemes.
He dreams of acorns, vast and grand,
While chatting with ants to form a band.

A crow caws loudly, 'Let's take to the skies!'
While critters beneath roll their beady eyes.
"Just stick to the ground, you feathered old fuss,
While we raid a picnic, it's all about us!"

The branches sway to their hidden delight,
As a bushy-tailed host prepares for the night.
But the rapscallion chipmunks, all dressed in stripes,
Steal all the snacks, forming giggling gripes.

And if you listen, amidst all the noise,
You'll hear leafy laughter from woodland joys.
For nature holds secrets of humor so grand,
Reflections of fun in this leafy band.

Whimsy of the Verdant Tides

In a pond where the frogs practice their song,
A turtle joins in, saying, "This won't take long!"
With splashes and croaks, they create quite the din,
Who knew that croaking could be such a win?

Nearby, the lilies are giggling in blooms,
While dragonflies dart around like tiny loons.
They twirl above water, a dazzling sight,
Competing for laughs in a comedic flight.

"Ribbit!" says one with a wink of his eye,
"To hop or not to hop, that is the sly!"
While the cattails chuckle, swaying in jest,
They're the funniest jokes of the pond, no jest!

So join the green chorus, come take a dive,
In the whimsy of waters, feel so alive.
Where laughter and joy mingle, breezy and wide,
In the playful serenade of nature's great tide.

The Journey of Root and Sky

A dandelion dreams of being a tree,
"Let me reach clouds, oh so fancy and free!"
But the ground giggles, keeps it down low,
While worm friends whisper, "You're perfect, you know!"

The sunflower stretches with bold, bright attire,
As ladybugs flutter, saying, "You're on fire!"
With petals like sunbeams and leaves that confide,
They dance in the breeze, full of warmth and pride.

A vine climbs higher, eyes fixed on the stars,
While flowers in pots argue who drives the cars.
"Let's roll down the hill!" one pansy does call,
As friends tumble down, giggles sweeten the fall.

So journey with roots and let laughter abound,
In the quest for the sky, let joy be your sound.
For from soil to stars, oh how wild it sways,
In this zany adventure of green, let's parlay!

www.ingramcontent.com/pod-product-compliance
Lightning Source LLC
Chambersburg PA
CBHW071429130526
44590CB00064B/2547